A Poetic Quest for Faith

VOL. II

A Poetic Quest for Faith

VOL. II

Craig A. Garner

ISBN: 1-59571-082-5
Library of Congress Control Number: 2005929706

Word Association Publishers
205 5th Avenue
Tarentum, PA 15084
www.wordassociation.com

Table of Contents

Foreword • 7

Creativity • 9

Broken Man • 11

Black Faces in High Places • 13

Stress Related • 16

Style over Substance • 18

TATs? • 22

The Ticket • 24

Throwbacks? • 26

Waiting in Line! • 30

What Ever? • 32

Who's on the Money? • 36

Why You Should Join (the ABTE) • 38

Missing my Father • 40

Turn the Page! • 42

Walk Bys? • 44

What's Up Dog? • 46

Don't Wait Until it's Too Late! • 48

Hurricane Hell • 50

The Look • 52

Don't Believe the Hype • 56

A No Brainer? • 58

Commitment to the Community • 60

Planning Board Blues • 64

Honor Them by Living Honorably • 66

Ambitions Curse • 68

Credibility? • 70

Confused? • 74

Inspiration • 76

Irvington on the Move • 78

Regal Spirits are Calling • 80

Dedication to African American Women • 84

Greatest Mind of His Times • 86

Do You Feel Me? • 90

Shadows • 92

Making a Difference • 94

Choices • 96

Unconditional Love • 98

Never Too Much! • 100

Foreword

This book of poetry, which is my fourth, is dedicated to my family members who have supported me throughout the years and who have made this offering possible. First and foremost is my wife, Veleria Brown-Garner who means everything to me since she has always been in my corner with unconditional love. Of course I would not be here without my mother Mrs. Catherine Garner and my father Mr. Andrew Garner who both have since passed away but will live forever in my heart. Next are my sisters, Mrs. Eleanor Land and Mrs. Felicia Grey although they do live pretty far away. Both of them have given me spiritual support through their love even through the ups and downs of our lives. Then there was Audrey the eldest sister who unfortunately passed away before I had a chance to tell her that she was my initial inspiration to help me believe in myself. I also must thank those extended family members such as Uncle Levi, Uncle James Newton, Aunt Ruth, Aunt Nola and Aunt Anna B. Covington who have also moved on to the after life. And lastly, I am indebted to those family friends that have supported me and my family throughout the years such as John and Anita Robeson, Janice West, Ethel Davion, June Key, and Gil Bragg. I would also be remiss if I did not mention two dear friends that unfortunately passed away with such untimely deaths who were Priscilla Butts and Shirley Waller.

The title of this book "A Poetic Quest for Faith" captures the essence of my reason for writing this book of poetry. As an "old school" homie from an urban background, I've recently seen a number of disturbing new trends in my community and in fact the world. There seems to be a lot of what I consider to be twisted logic out there that is becoming prevalent in our culture and therefore in many of our minds. And I'm not just referring to rap music. There is something considered to be the hip hop culture that is somehow indifferent to the history and culture that I grew up with. The potential impact of this "new logic" is that a whole new generation of our children may come along and think that it's normal or worst yet the way it has always been.

Through my poetry I'm attempting to appeal to a higher order which is our faith in each other, our faith in our traditions and values, and our faith in someone greater than all of us. I believe there needs to be another voice that gives a different point of view regarding what's going on. I refuse to settle for the latest fad or mundane knee jerk responses to fashion or musical interludes. Sometimes there is a reason the way things were done in the past are still working today. In my humble opinion we don't need to throw the baby out with the bath water every time something new comes along. Sometimes we need to listen to the inner recesses of our minds and hear ourselves think. Life isn't always a party but it can be appreciated anyway if we only let ourselves appreciate its simple beauty. In doing so, I believe that we honor ourselves and in fact each other.

I would also like to give a special thanks to the Honorable Wayne Smith, Mayor of the Township of Irvington, who appointed me the Poet Laureate of Irvington.

I consider this to be a tremendous honor and look forward to serving him with distinction. As with the previous book "A Poetic Twist of Fate" I have inter-dispersed some quotes between the poems from some authors who's work I respect and pay homage to by sharing their wisdom within my book. Thank you for purchasing this book and I hope you will share it with others.

Creativity

What inspires anyone
to undertake a task?

When no one knows
how far it goes
or if it will even last?

What grabs at your soul
and screams to be let out?

Even though you're not certain
what it's really all about.

Is it your emotions or
just how you feel?

That make this undertaking
turn out so very real.

Is the pain you've experienced
part of this whole concept?

If it is will you be prepared
to go into some debt?

        Just to express yourself
        and finally be free.

        Just to share with the world
        your own creativity.

        There is a price one must pay
        to be true to oneself.

Even if what is created
may end up on the shelf.

But one cannot worry
about the final outcome.

And must seize the moment
more than anyone.

Broken Man

My primal urges
are screaming out.

But very few even care
what this is about.

For I yearn to be a man
with all of my faults.

I yearn to be myself
in spite of what's sought.

But what I'm faced with
day after day.

Is ridicule and comtempt
if I don't act a certain way.

    If I don't speak softy
    or control my needs.

    I will be banished to
    hell for trying to breed.

    Kicked to the curb for
    simply speaking out.

    Regardless of what
    I'm talking about.

    All of this for simply
    trying to be a man.

All of this for doing
whatever I can.

Not to be broken
and not to give in.

To societies infringements
on how I can win.

Black Faces in High Places

Black faces in high places
should begin to set us free.

Black faces in high places
with huge responsibility.

Judge and jury of our lives
in everything we do.

Giving vestiges of hope they'll
have an understanding view.

But if Thomas, Powell or Rice
don't see themselves as such.

We will never really gain
what amounts to very much.

> Since they perceive themselves
> as Republicans and don't care.

> If we ever make it
> or really get anywhere.

> So these faces in high places
> must be considered just that.

> And never be expected to do
> something cause they're black.

> Never be placed upon a pedestal
> just for being the only one.

Never be revered and paraded
in front of everyone.

Since they're not our heroes
if they simply take their place.

When their actions are killing us
and against the human race.

Strive to have moral excellence in all one does so no fault can be found in your character. For Maat - the way of Truth, Justice, and Righteousness is great; it's value is lasting and it has remained unchanged and un-equaled since the time of it's creator. It lies as a plain path before even the ignorant. Although wickedness may gain wealth, wrong-doing has never brought it's wares to a safe port. In the end, it is Maat, the way of Truth, justice, and Righteousness that endures and enables the upright to say "It is the legacy of my father and mother."

Maulana Karenga - The Husia

Stress Related

Feeling helpless since
there is nothing I can do.

To make my child
see a different view.

Feeling hopeless since
my job just let me go.

Said they had to do it
since revenues were slow.

Feeling sick from having
to deal with all this mess.

Tired and aggravated
from all of this stress.

> But I must go on
> cause I can't stop now.
>
> Since my children need
> me so I can't allow.
>
> For them to be hurt
> by the painful things.
>
> This crazy world has
> been known to bring.
>
> Forcing beautiful actions
> to be negated.

Just because my pain
is stress related.

I will survive this stress
and will never give in.

Too blessed to be stressed
and determined to win.

Style over Substance

Going to the salon
to get your nails done.

So you can be styling
in front of everyone.

With two tone streaks and
fake diamond stones.

Took over two hours to do
just to get in the zone.

        Spending thirty or forty dollars
        to have this done.

        Just so they'll look better
        than anyones.

        Worrying about the look
        of your finger nails.

        While brothers are dying
        and going to jail.

        While the kids are screaming
        for your attention.

        And doing some things
        that you can't mention.

        Crying broke every week
        even though you claim.

You don't have enough
money to get in the game.

I can't believe that so many
sisters are acting the same.

Choosing style over substance
and being vain.

Self knowledge is the basis of true knowledge. The Egyptian Mysteries required as a first step, the mastery of the passions, which made room for the occupation of un-limited powers. Hence, as second step, the Neophyte was required to search within himself for the new powers which had taken possession of him. The Egyptians consequently wrote on (all of) their temples "Man, know thyself".

Stolen Legacy

George G.M. James

TATs?

Images of love
or images of war.

Can know be seen
in your department store.

But not on counter
or on the shelf.

On somebody's person
to express their self.

Guys and gals with tattoos
galore.

Covering their bodies
with more and more.

Ink stained messages
or girl friends names.

That can't easily be removed
and may invoke shame.

Just because it's hip
or what's in style.

Some pain is endured
for just a little while.

Yet the images on the body
may last forever.

And no longer really
be considered clever.

Or no longer be relevant
to your life.

And a total embarrassment
to your wife.

Your skin is beautiful
as a quite lake.

It doesn't need to be changed
for goodness sake.

The Ticket

Many high school athletes
are dreaming the dream.

To have more money
than they've ever seen.

Hoping to receive their ticket
to escape the hood.

In the form of a scholarship
to a college that could.

Put their name in lights
with all the hype.

Helping them to get drafted
almost overnight.

> But this dream is flawed
> since it overlooks.
>
> The need for the athlete
> to hit the books.
>
> Or what may happen
> if they get hurt.
>
> Then have to sit out
> a season as a red-shirt.
>
> They think they're special
> and don't have to go to class.

Based on some physical skills
that will not last.

Based on tougher competition
than they'll ever know.

Since millions of others are trying
to get
where they want to go.

Throwbacks?

Jim Brown or Dr. Jays
number thirty-two.

Have become the latest
fad and thing to do.

Buying throwback jerseys
from various teams.

Are the things that fulfill
a young mans dreams.

Styling like this and
fronting like that.

With a retired players
jersey on your back.

> Spending hundreds of dollars
> just to look cool.
>
> But ending up feeling
> like a damn fool.
>
> Throwing back instead
> of looking ahead.
>
> Throwing back and
> possibly ending up dead.
>
> Over a stupid old jersey
> that cost a mint.

While many of us are struggling
just to pay the rent.

Given the magnitude of
what's happening out here today.

We need to throw ourselves forward
instead of throwing money away.

No people that laughs at itself, and ridicules itself, and wishes to God it was anything but itself ever wrote its name in history; It must be inspired with the Divine faith of our black mothers, that out of the blood and dust of battle will march a victorious host, a mighty nation, a peculiar people, to speak to the nations of earth a Divine truth that shall make them free. And such a people must be united.

W.E.B. Du bois Speaks

Waiting in Line!

What is it about
waiting in line?

That drives me completely
out of my mind.

Is it the lines length
or time it takes?

For one individuals
transaction to take.

I can't do anything else
except stand right here.

It's enough to bring
a grown man to tears.

        Is the darn line moving
        or what?

        Now I begin cursing the clerk
        and cursing my luck.

        Impatient as ever because
        there's never enough time.

        Yet here I am again
        stuck in another line.

        Why don't they hire enough
        people to do the work?

So I won't be standing here
looking like a jerk.

Where is the manager of
this place?

Cause I don't have a lot
time to waste.

Since I waited too long
and didn't plan.

Now I'm in a hurry
but stuck in quicksand.

What Ever?

There are thousands of words we
can choose to use.

And hundreds of ways
to phrase our views.

Yet we find ourselves spiraling
into a generation gap.

That doesn't even realize
where we've been at.

Thinking they're so sophisticated
and have their acts together.

Yet when asked a pointed question
responding with "what ever".

> "What ever" doesn't even
> begin to answer the query.
>
> And certainly should just
> make most of us leery.
>
> Since this fragmented answer
> just shows disdain.
>
> For the art of conversation
> that barely remains.
>
> It signafies where we are
> and just what we'll accept.

Just to move on or
get to the next step.

Without even realizing that
this diminishes our worth.

Since it gives more credence
to intolerances turf.

The problem that faces us almost 120 years after political emancipation Is the need for psychological emancipation. We have not regained our freedom because we have not learned to listen to the inner voice of ourselves. We still listen only to the ideas, interpretations, explanations, and directions that are given to us from outside of our communities.

The Community of Self
Dr. Na'im Akbar

WHO'S ON THE MONEY?

As we experience commerce
through our daily lives.

There is that one constant
that cannot be denied.

It's the value we place
on the cash in our hand.

It's the value we use
when judging a man.

But one thing is obvious
yet not so funny.

Is that everything depends
on who's on the money.

Are they people you respect
and hold in high esteem?

Or is it someone that was
dishonest and downright mean?

Are they symbols of greatness
through and through?

Are they someone that even
looks like you?

> Is our only concern
> what we can get?

When we go to the bank
to cash that check.

Or should we consider
what's being augmented.

When millions of others
are not even represented.

Why You Should Join (the ABTE)

Sometimes it's not as clear
for everyone to see.

That the places we have reached
today were paved for you and me.

By pioneers who fought the fight
and sacrificed careers.

By demanding to be respected
for their work and their years.

The African Americans who were
first to take their place.

Had to endure the slings and arrows
just because of their race.

        The corporate way was filled
        with many traps and holes.

        That could deter many of us
        from reaching our goals.

        But some of us persevered
        with patience and our faith.

        Just so those that follow us
        could finally take their place.

        The Alliance helped us build
        a solid bridge of hope.

So future generations could
climb the corporate rope.

So as you sit amongst the best
with pride and dignity.

Realize this trail was blazed for you
by some you'll never see.

Dedicated to all the trailblazers
who never reached their dreams.

Missing my Father

It's rough growing up
without my Dad.

And really makes me
feel very sad.

Since no ones there
to help me out.

Or teach me what being
a man is all about.

And no ones there
to take my back.

When I come under
a physical attack.

I miss my Dad
each and every day.

And wish he had never
run away.

> Leaving me and mom
> to struggle all alone.

> Without the comforts
> of a safe home.

> No one to show me
> how to ride a bike.

Teach me when to run
and when to fight.

I need direction
like anyone else.

And hate it when I
have to rely on my self.

So if you're listening
to this today.

Please come back home
and stay.

Turn the Page!

So many of us are living
in a self imposed cage.

Simply because we refuse
to turn the page.

Turn the page and
get on with our life.

Instead of wallowing in
self-pity and strife.

The past is relevant
to what we know.

But shouldn't inhibit us
from where we can go.

If we learned something
from a negative situation.

This can help take us
to a higher destination.

A new day awaits us
a new page is here.

So dry your eyes and
have no fear.

Of what awaits us
when we turn the page.

And unlock the door
to our self imposed cage.

Knowing ourselves is a fundamental aspect of assuming personal power and effectiveness. An essential job which cultures should perform is to teach people the knowledge of themselves. The way for parents to raise their children, the things that are taught in school, the rituals, holidays,and ceremonies which occur in a culture should all be directed towards developing the peoples knowledge of who they are.

The Community of Self
Dr. Na'im Akbar

Walk Bys??

Would you interrupt the pilot
while he was landing the plane?

Would you bother the conducter
while he was driving the train?

Would you walk into a court room
while it was in session.

Would you interrupt a techer
while she was teaching a lesson?

Would you try to ask a question
while someone's singing a song?

Or would you wait until she's finished
and ready to move on?

        If you respect these folks
        i.e., their need to get their jobs done.

        Then give me the same respect
        that you'd give anyone.

        I need to focus on my work
        just like all of them.

        Since I don't want to have to
        start all over again.

        So please give me my space
        and respect my time.

By understanding that you may
just have to get in line.

Give a call or send some e-mail
to let us know your needs.

So we can schedule time for you
that will help us both succeed.

What's Up Dog?

Three hundred years of suffering,
fighting and praying for each other.

Culminating with the self-denigration
of our sister and brother.

Equating ourselves to nothing
more than a bitch or a dog.

While greeting our friends
in a mundane mental fog.

Actually barking to prove
that this is a fact.

Is a terrible testimony to
where we are at.

      In the realm of self-hatred
      it is now very clear.

      That we still loathe ourselves
      in spite of our fears.

      That we fail to understand
      the power of words.

      On our children's minds
      based on what they've heard

            How long will we take it?
            How long will we fail?

To consider the cost
of our self-imposed jail.

The bars on our minds
must somehow be broken.

If we're ever going to change
the words that are spoken.

DON'T WAIT UNTIL IT'S TOO LATE!

Don't' wait until you need some help
to step up to the plate.

Join your block association now
before it is too late.

We need your help to come together
and organize our block.

So we will have political clout
and the strength of a rock.

To deal with most of our issues
and be an effective force.

To make sure that our community
stays on an upward course.

We've invested a lot of money
in our homes and our land.

We have to do what we must
do and finally take a stand.

So support your Block association
and improve your community.

If you want to gain respect
you must first have unity.

A Block association is
the fundamental key.

That allows a township to
rise above futile misery.

So come attend our meetings
and finally have your say.

If you want your community
to have a better day.

C. A. Garner – President
Park Place Block Association

Hurricane Hell

Everyone wants to know
if you're doing well.

After experiencing the fury
of hurrican hell.

One hundred and fifty mile
an hour winds raking your home.

While rain pours down upon
you and kills all your phones.

Darkness seeps in just to
cover this mess.

Which is ultimately just one
of Gods many tests.

A test of your faith
in what you believe.

A test in your faith
before you're relieved.

From the burdens of earth
and all the things you may seek.

Not realizing that you
must sow what you reap.

The power of God
is no match for man.

In spite of our ability
to move mountains of sand.

So as we wait out
the force of his hand.

We should pray that he'll
restore peace all over the land.

And forgive our transgession
in spite of ourselves.

Forgive our arrogance
and allegance to wealth.

The Look

You knew when you saw it
and nothing had to be said.

If you didn't want to get slapped
up side your head.

Your mother often used it
to intimidate you.

Into doing just what
she wanted you to.

Her brow would curl up
and her eyes would get narrow.

Then she'd look you up
down to put you over a barrow.

> Peering over them glasses
> with such disdain.
>
> That you'd want to get out
> even in the rain.
>
> Then she might shake her head
> like you were a lost case.
>
> And put her hands up
> over her face.
>
> Next thing you know she's
> asking God for help.

Before she has to get up
and get the belt.

The look wasn't easy
but you knew the deal.

Better straighten up
before the next meal.

It took an educational effort that was systematic, intensive, and unparalleled in the history of the world to erase these memories, to cloud vision, to impair hearing, and to impede the operational of the critical capacities among African Americans. Once reference points were lost, African Americans as a people became like a computer without a program, a space craft without a homing device, a dependent without a benefactor.

Asa G. Hilliard III

Don't Believe the Hype

If you don't feel that something
is really your type.

Then go with your feelings
don't believe the hype.

Because the hyperbole is all
today's things are all about.

Fake bling bling so you
better look out.

Shows about nothing
on prime time TV.

Everyone's focus is
on me me or me.

> News that skims the surface
> about what is really real.
>
> While fake, phony, fiends
> are made a big deal.
>
> It's enough to make you sick
> if you know what I mean.
>
> Like a ship in outer space
> that's running out of steam.
>
> Diamond stud earrings
> being bought for a child.

Even if the little lad is
always acting wild.

Oversized clothing that's
supposed to be in style.

Even though you can't run
in it for just a little while.

Gucci bags, belts, and shoes
over two G's a pop.

Everything that's glitzy
cost a whole lot.

A No Brainer?

Some get it quick
while others are slow.

Some never get it
and are never in the know.

Since some are considered
a slow learner.

While others are claiming
that it's a no brainer.

But brains are needed
for everything.

From how we walk
to how we sing.

        What's simple to you
        may be hard for me.

        But the brain has always
        held the key.

        To our reactions for
        good or bad.

        To those distractions
        that make us sad.

        So to claim a task
        requires no brains.

Is like claiming flowers
need no rain.

Nothings as simple
as it may be perceived.

Even if one can do it
in lightning speed.

Commitment to the Community

Dedicating ones life to
always helping others.

Striving to support
your sisters and brothers.

Just so they can build
a life worth living.

Based on caring, sharing,
and unselfish giving.

Putting in long hours
almost every day.

Patching up petty differences
that come your way.

With persistence and patience
to see all things through.

Never losing your focus
on what you're trying to do.

> Committed to the cause and
> committed to the community.
>
> Having faith in the lord
> but self righteous dignity.
>
> Hoping that we'll make it
> and climb that mountain top.

Never hesitating for a minute
and never gonna stop.

Looking forward to the day
when everyone understands.

That we're ultimately measured
by our footprints in the sand.

By infusing the African and African-American content in the curricula, We, in effect, reaffirm the inalienable right of African people to (1) exist As a people, (2) contribute to the forward flowing process of human Civilization, and (3) share with as was as shape the world in response to Our own energy and spirit.

Wade W. Nobles, Ph.D.
Infusion of African American Content
in the School curriculum.

Planning Board Blues

Site plan reviews and
minor sub divisions.

Variance approvals that may
require revisions.

Notices incomplete or
worst yet missing.

Leading up to motions
for the apps dismissing.

        Tons of paper work
        for all to wade through.

        If you want to have
        a very clear view.

        Changing zoning ordinances
        that flip the script.

        Just when you think
        that you understand it.

        Requests from the Council to
        approve Improvement plans.

        Requests from the residents to
        take a firm stand.

        Attorney presentations that
        seem to take all night.

Site plan visits that
don't even look right.

It's enough to drive you crazy
if you really care.

It's enough to drive you crazy
if you want to be fair.

Relying on experts to
explain the case.

While you're still trying
to get on first base.

Honor Them by Living Honorably

The air is thick with the anticipation
that something terrible is going to happen.
But you can't run.

The smell of death has begun to waif
through your nostrils.

As rotting corpes begin
to bake in the sun.

The fear of being blown to pieces
has grabbed at your throat.

But you can't leave your position
nor let down your peers.

Since you have taken an oath to
defend the United States of America.

And no matter what happens you will fight
until your last gasping breath.

You will live by the code of honor
and never give up.

> Waging a battle that may not seem
> like it can be won.

> Taking on enemy fire from
> everywhere and everyone.

> Disregarding the pain and anguish
> of being so far away from your family.

Wondering if you'll ever see the face
of your wife and child again.

Praying that you will return home
without some kind of medical condition.

With the everlasting hope that somehow
it will all be worth it...

Ambitions Curse

Are you driven by ambition
and it's curse on all?

Trying to make it to the top
while others fall.

Trying to win at any
and all cost.

Striving to be the one
that is the boss.

Stepping on toes or worst
someone's neck.

Leaving bodies everywhere
like a huge train wreck.

> It shouldn't always
> have to be about you.
>
> The cost of the many
> should outweigh the few.
>
> Since lives are destroyed
> by your selfish ways.
>
> And many are subjugated
> to intolerable days.
>
> Just because of your
> relentless ambition.

Another life is placed
in a negative condition.

This has to stop for
better or worse.

Else we're doomed to be
controlled by ambitions curse.

Credibility?

Do you believe in me
like I believe in you?

Or do you need someone else
to tell you what you should do?

Are you even comfortable
with this dark face?

Since it's the oldest one
in the human race.

Do you hedge when someone
has a different view?

Especially when they
don't look like you.

        Do you think that others
        just won't have faith?

        In the decisions made
        by a different race.

        Do you doubt their
        credibility even though?

        Many have more education
        than you'll ever know.

        If so what is
        to become of us?

Blocked by this invisible barrier
and left in the dust.

Based on your assumptions
of how we will do?

When a decision has to be made
for me and you?

Greeks stole the Legacy of the African continent and called it their own. And the result of this dishonesty has been the creation of an erroneous world opinion; that the African continent has made no contribution to the civilization...This erroneous opinion about Black people has seriously injured them through the centuries up to modern times in which it appears to have reached a climax in the history of human relations.

Stolen Legacy
George G.M. James

Confused?

Don't know why you
have such a strong reaction.

Based on an emotional
or physical attraction.

To the same sex
that's just like you.

Though you're too young
to know what to do.

It might be real
or may not last long.

It might be right
or it might be wrong.

But one things for sure
and this I know.

Is you don't have to
decide which way to go.

Before going down a path
that's not for you.

Before you've experienced
a different view.

You have to at least
give your self a chance.

To understand more about
life than happen stance.

To assess your feelings
for what they are.

To listen to your heart
before going to far.

It's not always about
a physical attraction.

And may only be
a temporary distraction.

INSPIRATION

Every time I see her
I say to myself.

That you are fortunate
to have your health.

Every day that I
just see her smile.

I realize that I need
to go that extra mile.

For we are blessed
more than we know.

And should praise his name
everywhere we go.

If we've been allowed
to have our health.

Even though we are always
asking for wealth.

Cynthia inspires me
to do my best.

Instead of worrying
about all the rest.

Since she never let's her
disability get in the way.

Of trying to have
splendid day.

Since she stays upbeat
and works her show.

By still getting out
and staying on the go.

I sincerely thank her
for being this way.

And wish her all the best
each and everyday.

Dedicated to Cynthia Desouza

Irvington On the Move

The dawn of a new day's upon us
a tantalizing time is here.

The time for celebration
and victory is near.

Since Irvington's ascending
to heights it's never been.

Where everyone in the township
is now poised and posed to win.

With Mayor Smith at the helm
the ship is right on course.

To arrive at the doorstep
of destinies source.

With new businesses and commerce
generated through out the town.

A positive outlook for the future
has become to abound.

Working with a cooperative Council
great things are getting done.

No longer need to point the finger
at a department or anyone.

New Bus Terminal, new homes,
and new Schools on the way.

Has made for a most momentous
and marvelous day.

For the township of Irvington
is clearly on the move.

For the township of Irvington
has finally found its groove.

So continue to support her and
do whatever you can.

To ensure that she makes it
her destiny's in our hands.

Regal Spirits Are Calling

Regal spirits are calling
brother Ossie Davis home.

Regal spirits are calling
but not on a phone.

For they loaned us this man
for eighty seven years.

So he could fill us with love
and move us to tears.

With a stature that surely
was befit for a King.

He epitomized the words
"Let freedom ring".

        His kingdom was Harlem, the stage
        or wherever he went.

        He would travel the world
        so we could all repent.

        Fighting for justice
        all over this land.

        Demanding respect
        for his fellow man.

        Acting accordingly
        in his special way.

Bringing us into his tomorrows
or last years yesterday.

Standing with Malcolm
or marching with King.

Brother Ossie and Ruby
would let their hearts sing.

Spike called him the Mayor
even though he was not.

Yet his roles and his eloquence
will never be forgot.

Return if you must
so as will everyone.

But rest with the assurance
that the job was well done.

There is an educational crisis in African American communities today. For at least a generation some parents have left the responsibility for the education of our young to a school system that is at best poorly prepared and at worst has little expertise in educating children of African ancestry towards freedom...Reclaiming the education of our young is within our capacity.

Dr. Adelaide Sanford

Dedication to African American Women

You are the mother of all humanity,
the black pearl of the world, the
most beautiful, intelligent, multi
shaded, complicated, sassy woman
that cannot be imitated nor denied.

Your very presence unnerves many
because of your courage and fortitude.

You have endured more pain than
most people can even imagine.

        And yet, you have somehow managed
        to be the embodiment of love.

        Managing to raise your children
        without the man who created them.

        Able to somehow smile when
        you know things ain't right.

        Holding on and praying for
        others all through the night.

        Using your woman's intuitions
        like a surgeon uses a scalpel.

        Peeling away all of the pretenses
        like someone peels an apple.

        Your silky, smooth skin, and soft voice
        has made grown men hush.

While the curves of your body
has made mountains blush.

Your energy is boundless
and has supported an entire race.

I see mystic rivers when
I look upon your face.

I'm so thankful you're here
walking upon this earth.

And have accepted the responsibility
of giving all of mankind birth.

Greatest Mind of His Times

There have been so many
great African minds.

In the past in the present
but within their times.

Granville T. Woods invented
more electronic things.

Than anyone else would
attempt to bring.

A self taught electrician
a black engineer.

At a time when most folks
were blinded by fear.

> At a time when many
> could not get a job.
>
> Or where systematically lynched
> by a crazed mob.
>
> Created his own company
> established his own place.
>
> Was a not only genius
> but a credit to his race.
>
> Over sixty patents
> of electrical inventions.

That benefited mankind
with unparalleled intentions.

From the Telegraph, to
an incubator or air brake designs

Granville T. Woods was an
extraordinary man of his times.

You shouldn't measure a school by the thickness of the carpet. You shouldn't measure a school by who a child sits next to. You should measure a school mainly by teacher expectations, and I believe that is the most important factor impacting academic achievement.

Jawannza Kunjufu - Critical Issues in Educating African American youth

Do You Feel Me?

I'm sensing some pain
don't know where it's from.

Seems like it's comin
from mostly everyone.

As I walk this land
and see folks unknown.

Seems like they just
want to be left alone.

        But I need some love
        and affection.

        I need hugs and kisses
        more than protection.

        Where is the love
        for our fellow man?

        Where is the concern
        all over this land?

        Do we think we can make it
        without each other?

        Or do we really need our
        sisters and brothers?

Like back in the day
when we spoke to everyone.

That we saw when we left
and when they'd come.

We hugged and laughed
about each others day.

Wished each other good tidings
and went our separate way.

I'm still feelin you
but are you feelin me?

Are we being all that we can be...
for each other?

SHADOWS

Like a large storm cloud
that looms across the sky.

I sat in the shadows
without asking why.

For your presence was great
and so overwhelming.

That I deferred my own dreams
so our visions were melding.

With the focus on you
everywhere that we went.

There was rarely any time
for my frustrations to vent.

Always on the go and
and always in demand.

Sometimes it was really
more than I could stand.

        For to be in the shadows
        of your friend or your mate.

        Is a perpetual merry go round
        with a blind date.

        Since no one notices you
        or what you can do.

And they really don't care
about your point of view.

But one day they will see
that I too have a voice.

That they actually had
more than one choice.

To get an opinion to
hear what I have to say.

On more than one occasion
in my special way.

Making a Difference

You know when someone has it
nothing needs to said.

It is so abundantly clear
to all of those being led.

Down the path of righteousness
to a stream of hope.

While so many others
try to find strength in dope.

Very few pick up this mantle
since this choice could cost.

Very few step up to the plate
since their life could be lost.

    Just for speaking up
    in a moment of doubt.

    Disregarding the fact
    that they may be singled out.

    Ignoring their fears
    and boldly stepping up.

    Taking on an awesome challenge
    that could severely disrupt.

    The status quo, pecking order
    of how things use to be.

Before we were liberated
and finally set free.

Having the courage
to do the right thing.

Irregardless of the pain
that this may bring.

To them, or their family,
to others they love.

Having faith in the master
from high up above.

Choices

If the world is ever
going to hear our voices.

Then we will have to
start making better choices.

To err is human
and to forgive is devine.

But when will we consider
if we're running out of time.

For over fifty years
we've had the chance.

For our minds and our lives
to thus enhance.

By pursuing and obtaining
the best education.

That we can afford in
the towns of this nation.

If the world is ever
going to hear our voices.

Then we will have to make
more effective choices.

By expecting the best
from everyone.

By valuing hard work
over having fun.

The choice is ours
for better of worst.

The choice we choose
can make our bubble burst.

And leave us with nothing
or no where to go.

If we made the wrong choice
and didn't know.

Unconditional Love

There is no deeper love
than a mother's for her child

Even when it's not returned
just for a little while.

       She so desperately wants all
       of her children to succeed.

       That she'll sacrifice her health
       and disregard her needs.

       Will overlook the flaws
       and always try to see.

       Some good inside a child
       that's given her so much misery.

She'll sacrifice her savings
and eventually her life.

Just to somehow hold on
while enduring all kinds of strife.

Crossing rivers that so many
would never come to bare.

Taking chances that so many
wouldn't even dare.

Holding firm when all seems lost
and never giving in.

To life's eternal challenges
that we find ourselves in.

For this unconditional love
I would simply like to say.

That everyday that we have life
should be considered Mother's day.

Happy Mother's Day!

Never Too Much!

As the sun sets on one of the
greatest male singing careers.

Try as I might I can't
hold back the tears.

For Luther was everything
we could have asked for.

Since he gave all he had
and then tried to give more.

His silky voice was superb and
his delivery so smooth.

That it would instantaneously
put you in the mood.

> A perennial back up
> who became a shining star.
>
> By blazing trails that no one
> had expected from afar.
>
> Singing love songs supremely
> while sharing the stage.
>
> With beautiful Diva's
> regardless of their age.
>
> He gave us a reason
> to believe in love.

If only for one night
we could fly like a dove.

He will surely be missed
here and now.

Since he's sung his last song
and has taken his last bow.

Dedicated to Luther Vandross
C. A. Garner 7/07/2005

About the Author

Craig A. Garner has been a resident of Irvington, NJ for over twenty two years. During this time he has been a community activist, president of the Park Place Block Association, former elected member of the Irvington Board of Education, an elected Democratic District Leader, West Ward Chairman of the Irvington Democratic County Committee, and Chairman/Member of the Irvington Planning Board. His latest accomplishment was to be appointed Irvington Poet Laureate by the Honorable Wayne Smith, Mayor of the Township of Irvington.

Prior to coming to Irvington, Craig and his family resided in Newark, NJ. He is an honors graduate of West Side High School, Essex County College and Kean College which is now Kean University. He has worked for a fortune 500 company over twenty four years as a programmer, system analyst, data architect, and quality assurance manager. While working in this corporate structure Craig began writing poetry as a therapeutic method of dealing with his environment and numerous issues. But eventually he began writing poetry to express his concerns to students at numerous Career Fairs regarding the impact of the information technology revolution on their career choices.

Over the last twenty years he has self published three books which are Rhymes for Reasons I & II and most recently "A Poetic Twist of Fate." His experiences working in corporate America while maintaining his roots to his community provided him with a unique perspective of life that has laid the foundation for many of his poetic expressions. However, his experiences during a tour of duty in the Air Force also molded many of views. He was stationed in Eglin Air Force Base near Pensacola, Florida for four years during the Vietnam war and traveled throughout the south as one of the stars on the Eglin Base Basketball team. The images of the "sixties" south has also left impenetrable impressions on him that has influenced his writings.

Lastly, his re-education via attending seminars held by the First World Alliance in Harlem, NY and going back to college to take Black History courses solidified his understanding of his history. This self knowledge led to the belief in himself and his people as a driving force in the universe that demands to not only make a difference in life but a sustaining impression in history itself. This underlying strength plus the support of his wife and family has given Craig the inspiration to continue to write and have "A Poetic Quest for Faith" in mankind's positive attributes. Craig is married to Veleria Brown-Garner, who is a math teacher, has two daughters, Michelle Amparbin and Tammirah, two brothers, two sisters and three nieces.